**NEVER HELPLESS!
NEVER HOPELESS!
NEVER POWERLESS!**

NEVER HELPLESS!
NEVER HOPELESS!
NEVER POWERLESS!

A Weekly Devotional Guide & Prayer Journal

OLIVIA GAIL LANE
Shay Cole

Creative Chameleon

Copyright © 2022 Olivia Gail Lane.

All rights reserved. No part of this publication may be reproduced, distributed, or transmitted in any form or by any means, including photocopying, recording, or other electronic or mechanical methods, without the prior written permission of the publisher, except in the case of brief quotations embodied in critical reviews and certain other noncommercial uses permitted by copyright law. For permission requests, write to the publisher, addressed "Attention: Permissions Coordinator," at the address below.

ISBN: 978-1-73789613-5 (Paperback)

Library of Congress Control Number: 2022918541

Front cover image by gfx__specialist.

First printing edition 2022.

Creative Chameleon
Goodlettsville, TN 37072
www.acreativechameleon.com

Acknowledgements

I would like to acknowledge those who were instrumental in creating this book. To all who prayed for me, supported me, and encouraged me, I would like to say thank you. It has been a journey and I thank God you were there with me along the way.

To the publisher, Shay Cole, and her company Creative Chameleon, I appreciate your hard work and dedication to this project. Thank you for walking me through this and assisting me with my goal of becoming an author. We did it!

To my father, Pastor Clemmon T. Anderson, who is now amongst the great cloud of witnesses. I am so grateful to have known the depths of your love, support, and blessing. Even now, I can hear you cheering me on and I am forever humbled to stand on your shoulders. Thanks for being my inspiration and for giving me the freedom to be the best Olivia Gail that I can be!

To my husband, Brian K. Lane, thank you for being the shoulder I needed to lean on. Thank you for going on the ride with me and helping me make it to the finish line. Your love is seen, felt, heard, and returned. Thank you.

To my team behind the scenes, I appreciate you so very much. Thank you to Tresa Callahan with Game Face Glam Space in Southfield, Michigan for my amazing game face. Thank you to

Adera Brown of Adera Brown Design for my stunning attire. Thank you to Sharrall Elle Byrd with Byrd Photography Group in Detroit, Michigan for my wonderful images.

CONTENTS

Week One	1
Week Two	3
Week Three	5
Week Four	7
Week Five	9
Week Six	11
Week Seven	13
Week Eight	15
Week Nine	17
Week Ten	19
Week Eleven	21
Week Twelve	23
Week Thirteen	25
Week Fourteen	27
Week Fifteen	29
Week Sixteen	31
Week Seventeen	33

Week Eighteen	35
Week Nineteen	37
Week Twenty	39
Week Twenty-One	41
Week Twenty-Two	43
Week Twenty-Three	45
Week Twenty-Four	47
Week Twenty-Five	49
Week Twenty-Six	51
Week Twenty-Seven	53
Week Twenty-Eight	55
Week Twenty-Nine	57
Week Thirty	59
Week Thirty-One	61
Week Thirty-Two	63
Week Thirty-Three	65
Week Thirty-Four	67
Week Thirty-Five	69
Week Thirty-Six	71
Week Thirty-Seven	73
Week Thirty-Eight	75
Week Thirty-Nine	77
Week Forty	79

Week Forty-One	81
Week Forty-Two	83
Week Forty-Three	85
Week Forty-Four	87
Week Forty-Five	89
Week Forty-Six	91
Week Forty-Seven	93
Week Forty-Eight	95
Week Forty-Nine	97
Week Fifty	99
Week Fifty-One	101
Week Fifty-Two	103

Week One

I Receive Restoration

Scripture:
Joel 2:25-27

Each of us must acknowledge that in this life we may endure some losses, experience some downfalls, and may have some outright disasters. Yet it is comforting to know that God has already provided precious promises for every circumstance. In this passage, God promises to restore what has been lost, wasted, and consumed. He is a God of restoration. So on this first week of the year, receive His restoration in every aspect of your life. There is much to look forward to, much to embrace, and much to accomplish as God restores whatever has been lost.

Declaration:
Today I receive restoration in every area of my life. I will participate in my restoration as God leads. Good things are ahead. Whatever has been stolen, destroyed, removed, or missing shall be restored, replaced, and deposited into my life. I am excited as the good things are on the way!

Prayer:
Thank you Lord for your promise of restoration. Thank you for being concerned about every aspect of my life. I choose to receive

restoration in my home, business, professional ventures, health, and relationships in Jesus' mighty name, Amen.

Personal Reflections:

_____
_____
_____
_____
_____
_____
_____
_____
_____
_____
_____
_____
_____
_____
_____
_____
_____
_____
_____
_____

Week Two

God Can Reverse Bad News

Scripture:
2 Kings 20:1–6

In our scripture of focus, Hezekiah was experiencing a severe illness. The prophet, Isaiah, came to him with a message from God. The message was not good news. The message indicated that Hezekiah's days were numbered. Hezekiah heard this news and responded immediately. He turned his face to the wall and prayed to ask for an extension. Hezekiah poured out his heart before God. Shortly after, Isaiah returned with another message from God for Hezekiah. God responded to Hezekiah's petition and granted a 15-year extension of his life. God also promised to bless his natural efforts. At this time, whatever you are facing, take it to God in prayer. He hears, sees, and knows what you are dealing with. He will come to your rescue. He is still granting extensions, exits, and expansions. Yours is on the way!

Declaration:
I choose to pray about everything that is going on in my life and in the lives of those who are connected to me. I receive God's grace, mercy, and favor for every extreme situation because nothing is too hard for God!

Prayer:
Thank you Lord, for hearing me when I pray. Thank you for reaching me when negative reports and messages are delivered. I thank you now that you will turn these situations around for me. I thank you and praise you now! I will tell others about your goodness in my life. Amen.

Personal Reflections:

Week Three

Celebrating Victories

Scripture:
1 Chronicles 16:31-36

It is always a good thing to recognize God's goodness and greatness especially after a serious challenge. The Psalmist and current leader of the Israelites wrote this passage after the ark of the covenant was brought to the tabernacle. It was, indeed, a time of celebration even though there were many unseen challenges ahead. At this juncture, David saw that it was necessary to celebrate at this milestone. So, he led the people into a time of reflection, worship, and celebration. David and the people offered up thanksgiving. After the celebration and worship they were prepared and ready for the next battle. Worship and celebration are necessary, not optional, components of a victorious life.

Declaration:
This week I will pause to celebrate God's goodness in my life. I will acknowledge and appreciate every victory and I will be ready to address whatever is on the horizon.

Prayer:
Thank you Lord for everything that you have brought me through. Thank you for the protection, provision, and presence. Thank you for every accomplishment and achievement. I celebrate

your goodness and faithfulness in my life. Therefore I am strengthened and looking forward to the next conquest. You will show yourself strong once again! Amen.

Personal Reflections:

_____
_____
_____
_____
_____
_____
_____
_____
_____
_____
_____
_____
_____
_____
_____
_____
_____
_____
_____
_____

Week Four

God Is My Carrier

Scripture:
Isaiah 46:3-4

As we embark upon a new season, we must assess and re-adjust our thoughts, behaviors, and attitudes in order to prevent the repetition of undesired outcomes that have hindered us in the past. We must acknowledge that in past times it is likely that we have independently carried too much. It is a wonderful thing to recognize that God is our carrier from birth all the way into our senior seasons. God has already promised to bear, to carry, to sustain, and to deliver. That is reason to rejoice and reposition ourselves as no longer the carrier but the carried.

Declaration:
I choose to release the responsibility of carrying everything for myself and those that I am connected to. I choose to allow God to carry me along with everything that I have been weighed down with. God is my carrier.

Prayer:
Thank you Lord, for appointing yourself as my carrier. Thank you that I do not have to be fearful or worried about all of the loads that I have been independently handling. I thank you that I can

rest and relinquish my cares to you because you can and will handle everything for me. I trust you with all of my cares. Amen.

Personal Reflections:

Week Five

I Came to Win!

Scripture:
1 Samuel 17:45-47

The stage was set. The odds were not favorable. David had already been sized up as the inferior, the defeated, and the automatic loser. From the surface, it appeared that David was defenseless and defeated even before the battle had begun. Yet David knew who he was in God. As a result, he approached the challenge against Goliath with strength, fortitude, and confidence. So this week, choose to be unbothered by the odds, the statistics, the projected failure, and the predetermined defeat presented by others. Choose to proceed to victory in the strength of the most high God. Your opponents don't always know who you are working with!

Declaration:
This week, I choose to ignore what things look like on the surface. I choose to disregard and ignore the words of those who have already counted me out and declared my defeat. I will surpass every underestimation. I will pursue my victories in the strength and power of God who is the mightiest warrior ever known. Amen.

Prayer:
Dear Lord, thank you for bringing me to victory through Jesus Christ. Thank you that I can be victorious even when I start out

as the underdog. Thank you for overcoming power. Thank you for making me the one who will walk away with the prize. Thank you. Amen.

Personal Reflections:

_____
_____
_____
_____
_____
_____
_____
_____
_____
_____
_____
_____
_____
_____
_____
_____
_____
_____
_____
_____

Week Six

God Says That I Am Special.

Scripture:
2 Peter 2:9-10

When you know who you are, you can rise above mediocrity and mere survival. You can embrace success, prosperity, and overall well-being when you know what God has intended for you as His child. Once you embrace that identity, you become unstoppable and unformidable. Tactics of intimidation, manipulation, and even rejection are simply ineffective when you are confident and secure in the identity that God has bestowed upon you.

Declaration:
I know who I am and who I belong to. I am a child of God and I choose to identify as part of the royal priesthood. I am special and I choose to embrace everything that comes with my identification package.

Prayer:
Heavenly Father, I give you praise for designating a new identity for me. Thank you for sending your son, Jesus to redeem me from the sin-filled identity. I can now walk in my place of elevation, prosperity, and favor. I choose to walk in all of the benefits of being Your child. Amen.

Personal Reflections:

Week Seven

Things Are Happening While I Wait.

Scripture:
James 1:2

Been waiting for something? Think it's taking too long? Well, guess what. It's time to get excited! It's time to re-discover your enthusiasm! The scripture says to count it all joy when you are experiencing trials and tests. However, when we are in the thick of things, it may be very challenging to experience or display much joy. The good thing is that your current tests and challenges can be very productive. Remember, patience is being developed, character is being manufactured, faith is being fortified, and maturity will soon be displayed. So rejoice! God is doing some great things in you while you wait!

Declaration:
I will rejoice while I wait and walk through challenging experiences with grace and poise. I will focus on the characteristics of God that are being developed while I wait.

Prayer:
Lord, sometimes it is difficult to wait when I am uncomfortable and in distress. I thank you for building things in me while I wait. I know that you are working things out for me, so I will give you thanks and wait patiently for my breakthroughs. Amen.

Personal Reflections:

Week Eight

But Now...

Scripture:
Isaiah 43:1-3

The selected passage of focus begins with "but now" indicating that something had taken place that was different than what was about to be described. The Israelites had experienced much adversity up to this point in the text, but God spoke through the prophet Isaiah to communicate those two powerful words. He reminded them that He is the creator, the one who had formed them. He spoke of their eternal relationship and covenant. Then God let His people know that no matter what has been, a new day is beginning. He spoke of a day in which the waters would not overtake them, a day when the fire would not burn or even scorch them. Your "but now" begins today.

Declaration:
I choose to walk in my "but now." What has happened in previous seasons is over. I will proceed knowing that God is providing, protecting, and preserving me for great things that are on the way.

Prayer:
Dear Heavenly Father, thank you now for declaring that "but now" in my life. Thank you for protecting me while I am in the fire or the floods. I receive your promise now that I will not be

consumed by either. Thank you for my new day. In Jesus' name I pray. Amen.

Personal Reflections:
_____
_____
_____
_____
_____
_____
_____
_____
_____
_____
_____
_____
_____
_____
_____
_____
_____
_____
_____
_____

Week Nine

There Is Nothing Wrong With Asking.

Scripture:
Matthew 7:7-11

So many times we are hesitant to ask for what we need or desire. When we are dealing with close friends, relatives, coworkers, or superiors we are often reluctant to make requests due to fear. Fear of what they will think or feel about us or our requests. The scripture lets us know that we have a great father. The ultimate father. We can ask without hesitation because He will always give us good gifts. So go ahead, ask. Seek. Knock and find. You will receive without criticism, without scoffing or scolding, and without shunning. Let God bless you simply because he wants to do so. After all, He loves you and that's just who He is!

Declaration:
This week I will readily ask, seek, and knock. I will not be hesitant to make my requests to God about every aspect of my life because my Heavenly Father is concerned about my entire life. There is nothing wrong with asking.

Prayer:
Thank you Lord for being the ultimate father. Thank you for responding to my request without judgment, criticism, or rejection. Thank you for your everlasting love that is extended and expressed

each and every day. Thank you for answering my requests in your perfect timing. Thank you for daily loads of blessings in Jesus' mighty name. Amen.

Personal Reflections:

Week Ten

I Am God's Choice.

Scripture:
Psalm 65:4

It's a wonderful thing to be chosen by God. Often we are looking for people in high places to choose us for positions, promotions, business dealings, and relationships . Still nothing compares to being chosen by God. The scripture says "blessed is the man you choose. Those who are chosen by God will be satisfied with the goodness of your house. " Sometimes we disqualify ourselves because of how we have followed from afar or we feel inadequate because of past mistakes or missteps. Yet God chooses us based on our connection to Jesus Christ. When Jesus is Lord of our lives, God chooses us to experience His blessing, His favor, and His goodness. Today, we accept all that He has for us without struggle.

Declaration:
This week I embrace the favor of God that rests on my life because God has chosen me. I will not disqualify myself because of anything that has happened in the past. I choose to receive God's favor and His goodness right now and always. Amen.

Prayer:
Thank you Lord, for choosing me. I choose to walk in your perfect world for my life. Thank you for reserving special blessings

and favors for me. I embrace all that you have for me. Thank you for pouring out your goodness in my life in Jesus' name. Amen.

Personal Reflections:

Week Eleven

They Are Not Really Getting Ahead.

Scripture:
Psalm 37:1-4

It often appears that those around us who have no heart towards God are succeeding, triumphing, and winning in every facet of life. The Psalmist David indicated that those suspected winnings are not so secure and are short-lived victories. The scriptures indicate that we must not be distracted by the appearance of evil doers, temporary progress, and advancements. We must put our focus and trust in the Lord and feed on his faithfulness and eventually we will experience and receive the desires of our hearts.

Declaration:
I will not be distracted by others who appear to be getting ahead, even though their hearts appear to be far from God. I will delight myself in the Lord and obtain all of the good things that He has designated for me.

Prayer:
Lord thank you for keeping me focused on you. I will not compare myself to others because I know who I am in you. I know what you have for me. I know what you've brought me through. Thank you for blessing me with long-term victories. Thank you Lord for your faithfulness. These and all things we ask in your name. Amen.

Personal Reflections:

Week Twelve

God's Plan Is The Best Plan.

Scripture:
Joshua 1:8-9

It is always comforting to know that God's plan is for us to have a good life. His desire is for us to prosper, to excel, and to experience His goodness on a daily basis. However, He does not exclude us from the process of creating a good life. As a matter of fact, His word provides directions for us so that we can work with Him in realizing the prosperous life that He has intended. It is up to us to meditate on His word, and to allow His word to be our roadmap in creating and living that prosperous life that He has planned.

Declaration:
The word of God is my standard and roadmap for life. I will meditate on it day and night. When I do that, I am assured that my life will be blessed and prosperous as God has originally intended.

Prayer:
Dear Lord, thank you for abundance. Thank you for guiding me towards the life you want for me. Thank you for giving me the tools I need to be active in my prosperity. God, thank you for your word. Thank you for giving your word as a roadmap to get me closer to the life you have planned for me. Amen.

Personal Reflections:

Week Thirteen

It's Time For Restoration!

Scripture:
Isaiah 61:6-9

Sometimes it is necessary to step out from under the umbrellas of past experiences and consequences of lapses in judgment. In the selected verses, God uses the prophet Isaiah to communicate to His people that the season of consequences and repercussions is over. He expresses this as they transition from the time of difficulty and depravity. He will now bring them into a time of restoration. You see, God is a man of His word. He never remits or recants. The Israelites were His chosen people. Therefore, He was obligated to ensure their recovery. You belong to Him too. So embrace His promises in spite of the temporary difficulties, developments, and even the consequences of your own actions. Embrace the identity of being "the posterity whom the Lord has blessed."

Declaration:
I will not succumb to the pain of past experiences. I will rejoice in the restoration the Lord has for me. I am grateful that the season of difficulties and repercussions is temporary and won't last long. I thank God that I belong to Him and He keeps me restored.

Prayer:

Lord, I thank you for bringing me out of unsavory situations. Thank you for transitioning me from the turmoil of life to the place of peace. Lord, I thank you for your faithfulness, deliverance, and grace. Thank you for not leaving me in the storms. Thank you for bringing me out of the shadows and keeping me in your presence. Amen.

Personal Reflections:

_____
_____
_____
_____
_____
_____
_____
_____
_____
_____
_____
_____
_____
_____
_____
_____
_____
_____

Week Fourteen

Gotta change my clothes!

Scripture:
Psalm 30:11-12

When we have missed the mark, we are clothed in a contrite disposition if our hearts are set to please God. As a result, we may be engulfed in dealing with the consequences of our disobedience, rebellion, or simply the pursuit of our own agendas. The word lets us know that the consequences of our choices are temporary; just for a time and a season. After our acknowledgment, repentance, and contrition; God then begins the process of restoration. When the process of renewal commences, He takes the sackcloth and clothes us with gladness. We can then go and complete His purposes with gladness.

Declaration:
I will quickly repent for any actions that are not pleasing to God. I accept His forgiveness and I forgive myself. Now I will proceed in obedience and will throw off the garments of remorse and put on the garments of gladness and glory.

Prayer:
Heavenly Father, I thank you for forgiveness. Thank you for keeping me even when I turned away from you. Thank you Lord for deliverance and mercy. I thank you for new seasons in life. Thank

you for new opportunities for growth. Thank you for filling me with your purpose. I ask that you continue to keep me clothed in gladness. In your son's mighty name, Amen.

Personal Reflections:

_____
_____
_____
_____
_____
_____
_____
_____
_____
_____
_____
_____
_____
_____
_____
_____
_____
_____
_____

Week Fifteen

God is in it for the long haul.

Scripture:
Isaiah 40:28-31

We get tired. God does not. We run out of strength. God does not. We get drained. God does not. Our fuel, patience, and ability to endure can run out. God's does not. The scripture lets us know that God replenishes us with strength and whatever else we need when we are dealing with opposition and problems that are not fixed quickly. He will then cause us to have enough power to mount up, to run, and to walk; even after we have been counted out. So, decide to keep moving. Decide to stick it out. Decide to endure for the long-haul because there will be no fainting since God's power is more than enough.

Declaration:
This week , I acknowledge that I have enough power in God. As a matter of fact, I have everything I need to excel, to mount up, and to keep moving. I will do that this week. I will not faint because God is with me for the long-haul. I will be victorious!

Prayer:
Thank you Lord for empowering and fortifying me with your strength. I can face every challenge in your power and your strength. Thank you for filling me with all that you are today. Thank you

now for the victorious victories that will manifest as I keep rising up. Amen.

Personal Reflections:

_____
_____
_____
_____
_____
_____
_____
_____
_____
_____
_____
_____
_____
_____
_____
_____
_____
_____
_____
_____
_____

Week Sixteen

Angels on Assignment

Scripture:
Psalm 91:11-12

Angels are often underrated and underestimated and insufficiently acknowledged. We have all experienced close calls of danger, destruction, and great damage. But for some reason, the situation did not unfold as anticipated. We can all recall episodes of angelic intervention that took place and prohibited what almost destroyed us. God dispatched angels that averted the fatal accidents or a demonic agenda to take you out. God deployed angels to delay and detain people to prevent collisions, damages, and complete destruction. The angels do so much especially when we put them on assignment when we pray. What are your angels doing today? Have you given them any assignments? They are waiting. God has given you angels to watch over you. Put them to work when you pray.

Declaration:
I am thankful for the hosts of angels that are working on my behalf. They are moving and removing things. They are locating and bringing things to me now. As I pray, they will protect, connect, guard, defend, facilitate, and intervene. My angels are keeping me in all my ways.

Prayer:

Thank you Lord, for sending your son Jesus to rescue me from sin and giving your angels charge over me. Thank you for angelic intervention in all of my activities and affairs. I will not fear because my angels are at work. Amen.

Personal Reflections:

Week Seventeen

I have a friend.

Scripture:
John 15:9 - 15

At times we all feel alone. Jesus told His disciples that they no longer needed to be detached from Him, as a servant would be. Jesus explained that His purpose was to cause their joy to be full because they, His disciples, would now have the opportunity to engage in a different level of relationship. He declared to them that He called them friend. You might feel alone and may not be able to find any earthly support. Remember that Jesus calls you His friend. Therefore you are never alone. You cannot find a better friend than Jesus Himself.

Declaration:
This week I will not focus on who is no longer my friend. I will not be distracted by those who don't know how to be good friends. I will focus on cultivating my friendship with Jesus and I will never be alone again.

Prayer:
Thank you Lord for being my true best friend forever! Thank you for promoting me from the level of servant to friend. It is a great privilege to have you as my everlasting friend. I trust you and

I am looking forward to the great things that we will experience together! Amen.

Personal Reflections:

Week Eighteen

Going to the Land of No Limits

Scripture:
1 Corinthians 2:9-12

It's a wonderful thing to realize that what God has in store is more than what you have ever dreamed of or imagined. Sometimes our decisions reflect that we have no idea of where God has intended for us to be. The good thing is, all we have to do is find out what God has prepared for us as we walk with Him. He reveals His plan to us as we follow His direction. So go ahead, choose to go deeper! Choose to go higher! Your potential is unlimited because of what God has prepared for you.

Declaration:
This week I decide to depart from limited thinking. I choose to pursue the deep things of God. I am leaving the shallow water. I choose to receive all that God has prepared for me.

Prayer:
Dear Lord, thank you for designating great things for me. Forgive me for settling for less than what you have in store. Forgive me for embracing limiting thoughts. Thank you for taking me to great places in you Lord. Thank you for unlimited grace and favor. Amen.

Personal Reflections:

Week Nineteen

God's Word Is Final

Scripture:
Hebrews 4:11-13

When nothing else works, God's word works every time. The scripture indicates that we can enter into rest knowing that the word of God is alive and powerful. We can rest in our "God said" because God's word hits the spot and is effective and efficient in every circumstance. His word also covers and includes every possible problem or dilemma. God's word is final and should not be excluded out of our daily experiences.

Declaration:
This week I will dwell on my "God said"! I will depend on God's written and spoken word which is efficient in all circumstances. I refuse to toil or worry. Instead, I will simply declare what God says over my life and over the lives of others.

Prayer:
Dear Lord, thank you for your word which gives me everything I need for every situation. Thank you for the instructions to rest in you and in your word. I thank you that your word is alive and is working on my behalf today. Amen.

Personal Reflections:

Week Twenty

There's A Miracle In The Works

Scripture:
1 Peter 5:10-11

There are moments in every person's life that absolutely require an unquestionable move of God. The situation is out of the boundaries of human intervention. It is in those moments that we often fail to detect and discern that God is setting the stage for a display of His power. While we wait for a recognizable miraculous manifestation, we can miss the less obvious miracles that are taking place internally. God is demonstrating His power and presence in ways that are not visible to the human eye. The work that is happening inside of us supersedes any instantly visible occurrence that we could ever imagine or experience.

Declaration:
God is doing something big in my current situation. Every challenge in my life will be productive as God is perfecting, establishing, and strengthening me.

Prayer:
Dear Lord, thank you for working things out in my life. I thank you for handling every situation that I think is a crisis. My greatest problems are no challenge for you. While my miracles are on the way, thank you for working in me. Amen.

Personal Reflections:

Week Twenty-One

All You Need Is A Small Amount Of Faith

Scripture:
Matthew 17:14-21

A man with an epileptic son approached several of the disciples. He asked them to address the infirmity that caused his son to frequently jeopardize his own safety. The disciples were unable to deliver the young man from his illness. The disciples then brought the matter to Jesus. He fervently scolded them and clearly expressed that they could not address this sickness because of their own disbelief. Jesus provided some clear details in that moment of instruction, correction, and clarification. He told him that what they needed was faith the size of a mustard seed. So whatever you are facing, gather up a small amount of faith and deal with that mountain, that issue, or that crisis. You have enough faith to move it!

Declaration:
This week I choose to believe God. I refuse to focus on what I think may be lacking. I will use the small amount of faith that is necessary to conquer my latest challenges. I speak to the Mountains in my life and they will be moved.

Prayer:
Thank you Lord for my faith. I can trust you and your word! I have enough faith to obey your instructions in order to bring

changes in my life and in the lives of those who are connected to me. Thank you for moving the mountains as I exercise my faith. Amen.

Personal Reflections:

_____
_____
_____
_____
_____
_____
_____
_____
_____
_____
_____
_____
_____
_____
_____
_____
_____
_____
_____
_____
_____

Week Twenty-Two

God Fights For Me

Scripture:
Psalm 124 :6-8

All of us have encountered people who were classified opponents. The unfortunate reality is that everyone does not want to see you succeed. As a matter of fact, some have plotted schemes to facilitate your downfall. In those moments, which sometimes become whole seasons, it is comforting to know that God sees and knows about every single thing. He keeps excellent records. Even beyond that, He will not allow you to be destroyed by the enemy's tactics. Our faithful God is in the trap-destroying business. You can count on Him to come to your rescue every time.

Declaration:
God is my refuge and my help in the time of trouble. He will dismantle and destroy every snare and evil mechanism that has been designed for my detriment. God is my defender. He fights for me.

Prayer:
Dear Lord, thank you for being so faithful and consistent. I am thankful that I can count on you, especially in the midst of those who would like to see me fail. Thank you for being my mighty warrior and rescuer. You are my defender. You are a great God, so I will trust you in all my ways. Amen.

Personal Reflections:

Week Twenty-Three

I Speak To Things And They Move.

Scripture:
Luke 17:5-6

The disciples made a request to Jesus to increase their faith. In response, Jesus instructed them to use the power and methods they already possessed. When is the last time that you have spoken to an inanimate object? What have you spoken to? Have you called in that new job? Have you spoken to the door that you are waiting to open? Have you called in those new friends or those destiny helpers? Have you commanded your resources to come in from every direction? Have you called in your healing? You are human and as a result, have needs that need to be met. So, whatever it is, decide right now to use what God has already given.

Declaration:
This week I'll call in my (*Insert your need*). I receive all that God has destined for me. All blockages and hindrances are removed now in Jesus' mighty name. I choose to exercise the power that I have already been given. I speak to my (*Insert your need*) and call it in now.

Prayer:
My father, I thank you now for those blessings that I desire and the blessings that you already have in store for me. Thank you for giving me the power to speak to inanimate objects and

circumstances. Thank you for the changes that will be evident in Jesus' mighty name. Amen.

Personal Reflections:

_____
_____
_____
_____
_____
_____
_____
_____
_____
_____
_____
_____
_____
_____
_____
_____
_____
_____
_____

Week Twenty-Four

Someone Carries Me

Scripture:
Hebrews 4:14-16

Have you ever asked yourself why you are carrying any or all of your concerns alone? Ask yourself that question right now. What am I doing with all of this worry? It's not even necessary! You might as well continue that conversation with yourself. Help is available. You have a high priest who is able to empathize and sympathize. Handling things alone is not the way to proceed. Decide to run to the throne of grace and get some help. You can always get mercy and grace to help carry your loads.

Declarations:
This week I will not carry my concerns in my own strength. I will go to my high priest because He understands everything that I am dealing with. I do not have to walk alone because I am not alone. Jesus will carry me and my loads.

Prayer:
Dear Lord, thank you for ensuring my success by making provision for my blessings. Thank you for handling everything that concerns me. I am so glad to know that help is always available. So I receive your mercy, grace, and favor to help me right now in Jesus' mighty name. Amen.

Personal Reflections:

Week Twenty-Five

Some Voices Must Be Silenced.

Scripture:
1 John 4:1-4

Since biblical times, many voices have spoken. Many voices are still speaking even now in all kinds of platforms and forms of media. Messages are being sent from every direction. However, every voice that speaks is not of God. Negative voices can speak through individuals that are closest to us. Those voices are often the loudest and most penetrating. It is our task to be able to distinguish which voices and messages deserve our attention and space. It is good to know and remember that God is greater than any voice that opposes His plan for our lives. Thankfully, the Holy Spirit guides us in every situation so that we can distinguish which voices are speaking God's will for our lives. It is a good thing that we can choose, so we must choose wisely.

Declaration:
This week I will be at peace because God is greater than any opposition. I will not be confused about what voices and messages are the right ones to follow. The Holy Spirit will guide and lead me through every challenging experience.

Prayer:
Dear Lord, thank you for making it possible for me to avoid confusion. Thank you for leading me through every decision. Thank you for silencing every voice that speaks loudly and persistently tries to influence me to make choices that are contrary to your plans and desires for my life. I know that you will always take me to profitable outcomes. Thank you now great God, in Jesus' mighty name. Amen.

Personal Reflections:

Week Twenty-Six

I See It Differently

Scripture:
2 Corinthians 12:7-10

Learn to read things differently. It is a common occurrence to misread circumstances and think that whatever you are experiencing at the moment is the final state of the situation. We must decide and remind ourselves that there is something bigger and better in the works. God is doing something while you are walking through that crisis. Every problem can be a powerful opportunity for great productivity. Something good and magnificent is being established. God is perfecting you while you walk through the affliction. Something great is on its way!

Declaration:
This week I will look forward to the greatness that is on the other side of my adversity. I know that my miracles are in process and God is doing something in my crisis. So I will endure for Christ sake. For when I am weak, through Christ, I am made strong.

Prayer:
Dear Lord, thank you for using my crisis to produce miracles. I thank you for demonstrating your power and grace on my behalf. I am excited about the aftermath of my current situation. I already

know that my miracles are in process. Thank you for all that you are doing in Jesus' mighty name. Amen.

Personal Reflections:
_____
_____
_____
_____
_____
_____
_____
_____
_____
_____
_____
_____
_____
_____
_____
_____
_____
_____
_____
_____

Week Twenty-Seven

God Never Lies

Scripture:
Hebrews 6:17 - 20

In those moments when it seems that your hope escapes you, remember one thing. It is impossible for God to lie. Ever. We can receive consolation in the midst of uncertain circumstances. God has made some promises which he will not recant. He has made provision for our hopes, dreams, and His promises to be realized by way of Jesus Christ. Therefore, we must resolve that our hope will consistently defy logic. We can also resolve that our hope in God's specific promises to us will always carry us far beyond what our natural eyes can see.

Declarations:
This week I choose to retrieve and retain my hope. No matter what comes or goes, I always have hope. I can and will make it through anything because my hope is unmovable and unformidable.

Prayer:
Thank you Lord, for making a way for me to have hope. Since Jesus is my Lord, I know that the adverse circumstances are temporary and any obstacle will be removed. Thank you for giving me so much to anticipate. Thank you for everything that is in my bright and exciting future. Amen.

Personal Reflections:

Week Twenty-Eight

The Judge Has Been Dismissed

Scripture:
Matthew 7:1 - 5

As we mature on our journey with God, we must realize that it is not beneficial to express every thought that comes to mind about others. One of the biggest traps that we can fall into is judging others. We draw conclusions, make decisions, and determinations based on faulty and incomplete information. That behavior never works in our favor. The scripture explains that it is best to avoid being judgmental and critical of others, especially when we have our own issues to deal with. So we must refrain from hurtful judgments and criticisms and direct our attention to personal concerns of our own and address those.

Declarations:
This week I choose to refrain from criticizing and judging others. I will focus my attention on the areas that I need to address in my own life. I will use my words to edify, support, and encourage.

Prayer:
Lord, thank you for surrounding me with people who will not judge, but will assist and support me. Help me to be that kind of person to others. Show me how I can help and support without criticizing or judging others. Thank you, Amen.

Personal Reflections:

Week Twenty-Nine

Nothing can stop me unless I let it

Scripture:
James 1:12-15

Every day we are confronted with opportunities to stray from the path and plans that God has designated for our lives. The distractions and temptations appear to come from innumerable directions. We are instructed to endure temptation. That instruction also comes with a promise. We will be blessed when we avoid and endure temptation. You see, we have an enemy who does not want us to accomplish our goals. We have been given power and authority over our enemy and ourselves. We must decide not to be moved by fleeting temptations and distractions. We must pursue and accomplish. We must decide to be unstoppable.

Declarations:
This week I declare that I will not be pulled off course by activities, things, or people that bring temporary and immediate gratification. Instead I will decide to be unstoppable, focused, and unmovable. God's plans for me will be realized.

Prayer:
Dear Lord, thank you for having great plans in store for me. I choose to embrace my wonderful future. In the meantime, I will continue to resist temptations and I will pursue all that you have

intended for me. Thank you for depositing and birthing greatness in me, in Jesus' name. Amen.

Personal Reflections:
_____
_____
_____
_____
_____
_____
_____
_____
_____
_____
_____
_____
_____
_____
_____
_____
_____
_____
_____

Week Thirty

Preparing For Restoration And Recovery

Scripture:
Job 14:7-9

It is time to decide that recovery shall happen in your life. The illustration of a tree that has been cut down but has the capacity to bring forth branches again should remind us that recovery is possible. We must recognize and invite renewal after affliction. After all, affliction prepares us for restoration. So we should never lose heart. Instead, simply embrace and prepare for recovery, renewal, and complete restoration.

Declaration:
I decide that with the grace of God, I shall recover from whatever has taken place in my life. I refuse to be counted out. I refuse to be defeated. I refuse to believe that what I am experiencing now is all there is. With God's help, I am coming back! Restoration, renewal, and recovery belong to me in Jesus' name!

Prayer:
Dear Lord, thank you for changing my perspective about past events in my life. Thank you for helping me to see that the adversities and afflictions have purpose. Thank you for creating fertile ground for personal growth and development. I thank you now for restoring whatever I have lost. Amen.

Personal Reflections:

Week Thirty-One

Hey Everybody, I Am Blessed!

Scripture:
Proverbs 10:22

Have you ever felt like you were ashamed of being blessed? Have you ever tried to hide or diminish your blessings because of how you thought someone else would react? It is unfortunate, but many of us have even done things to avoid being blessed. It is time to make a major adjustment. The word tells us that God wants to bless us lavishly and that true blessings come without sorrow. So stop wrestling, refusing, delaying, sabotaging, diminishing, denying, refusing, or hiding your blessings. Decide right now to embrace and receive all of the wonderful blessings that God wants to pour upon you in this season.

Declaration:
I am blessed by my Heavenly Father. He has designed tailored gifts just for me. I refuse to exert any effort into sabotaging, diminishing, or even minimizing my blessings to accommodate others. Instead, I will gladly and graciously receive my blessings so that I can then bless others. God has blessed me and is blessing me right now to the point of overflow. I will never be ashamed of my blessings ever again.

Prayer:

Thank you Lord for blessing me! Thank you so much for intentionally ensuring that I experience your goodness in every aspect of my life. Forgive me for minimizing or rejecting your blessings. I choose to humbly receive your unending grace and favor in my life, in Jesus' matchless name. Amen.

Personal Reflections:

Week Thirty-Two

It's Time To Turn The Page

Scripture:
Joshua 5:9

There are things in our lives that we wish we had never done. There are places that we regret ever stepping our feet in. There are words that should have never been spoken and certain deeds that should have never been executed. Yet, it really did happen. Often times we get stuck in those moments and memories. We get stuck rehearsing the 'what if I had never' speech. The truth is there is nothing that we can undo, unspeak or unstep. The good news is that even when we are experiencing consequences that follow foolish actions, God is yet merciful and pronounces that the reproach (the shame, guilt, embarrassment, reproof, displeasure, and disappointment) shall be rolled away. We don't have to pay for the errors and rebellion forever. With Jesus, we can let that shame go! Let God roll it away!

Declaration:
Whatever has brought me to shame is being removed and resolved. God is rolling away the reproach in my life. I am forgiven and I will forgive as needed. I will not live in shame and regret any longer in Jesus' name!

Prayer:
Thank you Lord for making it possible for me to live a blessed and prosperous life without shame and guilt. Thank you for sending Jesus to pay for all of my offenses. Since the price has been paid, I can walk in freedom and blessing shamelessly. I receive all that you have for me in Jesus' precious name. Amen.

Personal Reflections:

Week Thirty-Three

I Am Done With Worry!

Scripture:
Matthew 6:25-34

Many of us have proceeded into adulthood being influenced by champion worry-ers. It was not intentional, but many have been literally taught to worry. It was simply a way of life. It was thought and communicated inadvertently that if you didn't worry you were too confident, arrogant, prideful, or simply full of yourself. Yet the reality is that worry is not from God. It is based on pure fear. Worry stirs up and feeds insecurities, doubt, and unbelief in oneself and in God. There comes a time that we must decide to depart from those things that hinder us and our contrary to the word of God. So even though you have been wired and disciplined by some of the best worry-ers, it's time to let all of that go. Don't be a worry-er. Instead be a prayer warrior! Seek the kingdom of God and you will find that you really don't have space for worrying.

Declaration:
I choose to seek the kingdom of God and His righteousness. I refuse to allow doubt, fear and disbelief to be present and evident in my life. My Heavenly Father will meet all of my needs. Instead of worrying, I choose to pray, knowing that my Heavenly Father knows all of my concerns and He will address them as He sees fit. My worrying days are over!

Prayer:
Dear Lord, thank you so much for releasing me from worry. I thank you for the opportunity to simply rest in you. I am grateful for all of the blessings that you are providing in every aspect of my life. I choose to trust you to meet every need. I know you will come through for me every time. I thank you now. In Jesus' name I pray, Amen.

Personal Reflections:

Week Thirty-Four

My Words Expose Where I Dwell

Scripture:
Psalm 89:10-12

In this day of multimedia communication, most of us are keenly aware of the power of words. Messages are sent and received through various platforms. Regardless of the means by which we communicate, one thing is true. Words have power. Words tell so much. Words are used to communicate feelings, thoughts, commitments and so much more. In our selected passage, the psalmist writes and expresses the value of being in God's presence. He expressed his commitment and devotion. The Psalmist clearly communicates and tells where his heart is and it is with God. You see, your words expose where you are, where you settle, and even where you hang out. It is obvious when you open your mouth, when you write, text, or use any other method of communication. The best place to dwell is in the presence of God. We lack nothing in His presence and we never have to leave. Remember, your words tell where you dwell.

Declaration:
I will be aware that my words indicate where I dwell. I will be conscious and aware of my spiritual location. I choose to dwell in God's grace, goodness, and favor. I will dwell, linger, and abide where I am loved, covered, and where I have everything I need.

Prayer:

Thank you Lord, for being my sun and shield. Thank you for giving me grace and glory. Thank you for making your presence a safe place for me to dwell in. I thank you for being my safe place and my refuge. I thank you that my friends, family, and other associates will clearly see and hear where I dwell because my words will clearly display that I am with you. Amen.

Personal Reflections:

_____
_____
_____
_____
_____
_____
_____
_____
_____
_____
_____
_____
_____
_____
_____
_____
_____
_____
_____
_____
_____
_____
_____
_____

Week Thirty-Five

How Are You Running?

Scripture:
1 Corinthians 9:24-27

Each day that we live we should have some kind of goal in mind. If we don't, we will find ourselves moving through life without much accomplishment. In this passage, the apostle Paul wrote to the Corinthian church and the rest of the modern-day believers. He used the illustration of a runner who is engaged in a race. He admonishes us to not just run but to run to win the prize. He elaborates and makes it personal saying that he is not running with uncertainty. Winning requires discipline in every aspect. You can't start and stop or take multiple side trips and expect to win. You may finish, but being the winner becomes a less likely option following persistent distractions. So decide now, that whatever you are working on will be completed. Decide that you will be the best that you can be in your assigned race. Run to win!

Declaration:
I have goals. I am not just engaged in aimless activities. I am not just doing busy work. I have a purpose. I seek God and He reveals the best strategies. I will finish and complete the task before me because I am disciplined in every area of my life. Losing, quitting, and forfeiting are not feasible options. I am a winner!

Prayer:

Dear Lord, thank you for making it possible for me to win. Thank you for sending your son Jesus to pay the price for my victories in every aspect of my life. Thank you for giving me access to everything I need to win. I ask you for your help in those areas that I have not been disciplined in. I know I can do it as I depend upon all that you are. I thank you now for victory in every area of my life, in Jesus' mighty name, Amen.

Personal Reflections:

Week Thirty-Six

Moving To A Healthy Place

Scripture:
James 5:13-16

All of us at one time or another have experienced some type of sickness or brokenness. We have all experienced the situation in which something needed to be fixed. Something has been off-balanced, missing, or malfunctioning in the emotional, mental, and physical realms. The good news is that there is no need for us to stay in an unhealthy place. The scriptures tell us that healing in every aspect of our lives is available. We do not have to succumb to the aftermath of various illnesses that show up in the form of physical, emotional or mental diseases. Jesus died for our healing and God has provided clear steps for us to access the healing that has already been purchased for us by way of Jesus' death, burial, and resurrection. Pray and receive healing. Call others who will pray with you. Whatever you do, don't settle in an unhealthy place, because healing is available for you.

Declaration:
I acknowledge that I have been experiencing symptoms of sickness. I choose to receive healing now. I forgive those who have hurt me. I forgive myself for past mistakes. I receive healing in every aspect of my life. I choose not to stay in unhealthy environments and relationships. I am moving to a healthy place.

Prayer:

Heavenly Father, thank you for making a way for me to be healed in my body, my mind, and my spirit. Thank you for healing everything that is broken. Thank you for replacing everything that has been lost or missing. Thank you for healing me from the past. I can now move forward because I am healed! I thank you now in Jesus' mighty name, Amen.

Personal Reflections:

_____
_____
_____
_____
_____
_____
_____
_____
_____
_____
_____
_____
_____
_____
_____
_____
_____
_____
_____
_____

Week Thirty-Seven

I Will Have A Story And I Will Tell It!

Scripture:
Philippians 4:19

There are times when you wish your life was different. Periodically, we all desire to have less opposition, fewer challenges and smaller hurdles. The reality is, if we have no opposition, our lives will be void of opportunities to grow and develop. We would miss the occasions to develop our trust in God. We would miss the chances to tell our children and their children of the many experiences of how God did phenomenal things for you. Then those generations would have nothing solid to build their own faith on. So look around at your current situation. Take inventory and see all of the testimonies that are in progress. Decide that when it all turns out the way God intended, and even along the way, you'll tell the story! That's right! You already see that God is meeting your needs. He is sustaining you through all of the challenges. So decide and refuse to allow those opportunities to go to waste. Praise Him on the journey and tell the story! God will get the glory!

Declarations:
I will choose to see every challenge as an opportunity for growth. I expect the challenges of my life to become more and more difficult. The increased difficulty indicates that I am growing. So I will not

sweat or fret. I will prepare to testify of God's goodness in my life. I will tell the story and God will get the glory!

Prayer:

Thank you God for promising to meet all of my needs. I will not be anxious about circumstances that are beyond my control. I will rest in you and your promises. Thank you for past victories. Thank you for the stories that are in progress right now. I will testify and my life will be living proof of your goodness, in Jesus' name, Amen.

Personal Reflections:

Week Thirty-Eight

We Already Know!

Scripture:
Deuteronomy 20:1-4

In the New King James version, this scripture begins with the word "when", implying that conflict was imminent. God was providing preliminary guidance and direction concerning how the Israelites were to approach and proceed in this uncomfortable part of their journey. He told them how they were to enter into the conflict, even when they were outnumbered, having what appeared to be insufficient weaponry, and being outright overpowered. God clearly told them that they should not be afraid or terrified because He would go with them to fight against their enemies. It is the same for us today. There may be intimidating people, circumstances, and developments. We must know that God has already made provision for our victory. When He sent His son Jesus, and He went through the entire death, burial, and resurrection; our victory was secured. So no matter what the looming threat may be, we already know that the outcome will be our victory. So proceed into the next challenge, knowing that victory is imminent! Go in like you already know how this thing is going to turn out. Present and carry yourself like you understand and know who is fighting for you.

Declaration:

I will not walk in fear regarding any situation. I am not afraid of people or any other kind of threat. I will not be intimidated or talked out of the outcomes that God has designated for me. I am victorious in every aspect of my life.

Prayer:

Thank you Lord for fighting for me to defeat my enemies. Thank you for sending Jesus who complied with your plan. Thank you for the completion of the death, burial, and resurrection of Jesus that allows me to walk in victory. I will not be defeated in Jesus' mighty name. Amen.

Personal Reflections:

_____
_____
_____
_____
_____
_____
_____
_____
_____
_____
_____
_____
_____
_____
_____
_____
_____
_____
_____
_____

Week Thirty-Nine

I Am Blessed For A Reason

Scripture:
Galatians 6:7-9

Many times we pray and ask God to bless us to ease our own discomfort in some aspects of our lives. We ask for a new house so that we can have more room. We ask for a car so that our transportation can be more comfortable and without incident. We ask for financial increase so that our personal pressure and stress can be relieved. Truth of the matter is, there are other reasons that God blesses us with our desires and His own desires for us. God does want to bless you. He does want you to have nice things. He does want you to be healthy and to have more than just enough to meet your needs. He wants to bless you so that you are able to bless others. So that house is not just about you. That new job is not just about you. The next breakthrough that is on its way is not only about you. There is a purpose in every blessing. God has added promises to being a blessing to others. He says that as we bless others with tangible and intangible gifts, we will also reap in abundance. He promises to multiply and cause us to overflow in His goodness. We must literally expect blessings so that we can then share them and bless others. Who will you bless this week?

Declaration:

I rejoice because God is good to me each and every day. Even at my lowest point, I always have something to deposit in someone else's life. I will not miss opportunities to bless others. I am receiving my harvests every day. So I will not be discouraged or disheartened. My harvest is happening right now.

Prayer:

Dear Lord, thank you for blessing me with so many good gifts. Thank you for allowing me to speak an encouraging word, share a smile, or help someone pay a bill. Thank you for the ability to pour into others lives. I realize that I will not like anything when I am diligent and blessing others every day. Thank you for my harvest. Thank you for blessing me for a reason. Amen.

Personal Reflections:

_____
_____
_____
_____
_____
_____
_____
_____
_____
_____
_____
_____
_____
_____
_____

Week Forty

Change Happens In Abiding

Scripture:
1 John 2:1-6

Sometimes we think that things and people are the way they are permanently. It is so good to know that each day we choose to walk with God, He is changing us. If we allow Him to do so. The scripture says that as we keep God's word, His love is perfected in us. It is comforting to know that God is constantly working on us as we live in Him. It is not His intention to leave us the way we are. However, we do realize that the changes may not always be comfortable. As a matter of fact, we often cling to the characteristics, traits, and behaviors that are not becoming. The process of releasing those elements is often through adversity and difficult situations. It is also those difficult moments that we have tendencies to become indecisive or make excuses. If we choose either of those options, we will miss the outcomes that are necessary and rewarding. So let's decide to dwell and abide in Him. Let's allow God to perfect His love and all that He is in us. Let's agree to change and to be changed. It's the only way to win!

Declaration:

I am changing in a good way. I am becoming more like Christ and less like the me that I know. I am growing each and every day as God's love is being perfected in me. I am not going anywhere away from God. I choose to dwell and to abide in Him. I refuse to make any excuses for imperfection. God's love is being perfected in me each day.

Prayer:

Dear Lord, thank you for consistently shaping and molding me. I am grateful that I do not have to stay the way I am. Thank you for perfecting your love in me. I am secure in you and I choose not to leave or to make excuses when I fall short. Thank you for your grace and mercy that is abundant in my life each day. Thank you for changing me so that my life brings glory to you. Amen.

Personal Reflections:

Week Forty-One

Never Hopeless!

Scripture:
Romans 15:13

In this time of uncertainties; with the pandemic, war, unanticipated job changes, the great resignation, and all kinds of cultural developments, we've all faced some transitions we never anticipated. Many have experienced unexpected losses of loved ones, drastic changes to financial resources, and other interruptions of security and stability. It is comforting to know that God has provided a way for us to be replenished on a continuous basis. He is the source. The scripture indicates that God is the God of hope and it is His desire for us to be filled with all that He is, no matter what our fluctuating circumstances look like. It is God's will for us to not only have hope, but to abound in hope by the power of the Holy Spirit. It is our responsibility to receive and activate that hope. Embrace the notion that you always have hope. Not just a dribble or a splattering, but you can abound in hope at all times!

Declaration:
I decide to receive and walk in the everlasting hope that God provides. He is my hope. He gives me hope. I can and will abound in hope because the Holy Spirit is my power source. I am never hopeless!

Prayer:
Dear Lord, thank you for being my hope. Thank you for making provision for me to always have hope through and in Jesus Christ. Thank you for empowering me by way of the Holy Spirit, who is my power source. I receive all that you are and all that you will do in my life. I thank you for abounding in hope, in Jesus' mighty name. Amen.

Personal Reflections:
_____
_____
_____
_____
_____
_____
_____
_____
_____
_____
_____
_____
_____
_____
_____
_____
_____
_____
_____
_____

Week Forty-Two

Preparing For The Finish Line

Scripture:
Psalm 34:4-6

It is a good thing to reflect upon what God has already done while we face the challenges of today. When we recount all of the battles that He has already brought us through, we can look forward with great expectations of the victories that are ahead. So when we agree with what God already has planned for us, we can prepare for the celebrations. We can get ready for the finish line. We can prepare for the hugs, salutations, rewards, and awards and innumerable expressions to celebrate our accomplishments. Get ready for your victory! Congratulate yourself in faith!

Declaration:
This week I will think about all of the victories that God has already brought me through. I will step over and around every distraction and deterrent that is presented to alter my course and steal my success. I will hear and receive the prize! So congratulations to me!

Prayer:
Thank you Lord for your promise that says I shall not lack any good thing. I praise you now for the completion of projects, tasks, and assignments. Thank you for the grace to complete and

accomplish what you have intended for me to accomplish, in Jesus' mighty name. Amen.

Personal Reflections:

_____
_____
_____
_____
_____
_____
_____
_____
_____
_____
_____
_____
_____
_____
_____
_____
_____
_____
_____
_____

Week Forty-Three

Faith Works!

Scripture:
James 2:17- 20

Let's face it. We all like the safe road. We enjoy being comfortable. Many of us prefer what is predictable. For some, more than others, we will usually choose options that are familiar with minimal risk. We must admit that when we cling to what is predictable and familiar, we frequently forfeit valuable experiences, increased prosperity, and fulfilling outcomes. The truth is, what is safe and predictable does not require faith. Faith requires risk. Faith requires releasing control of every single detail and variable. Faith requires proceeding without having all the answers. So the question is, are you choosing what is safe and predictable and forfeiting what really could be? Are you choosing or have you settled for what is familiar? Can you step out of the comfortable boat and believe God for what does not make sense to you or anyone else? The evidence will be that miracle, that breakthrough, that solution, or that impact in someone else's life. My faith is not dead. My faith works!

Declaration:
This week I will depart from what is comfortable and predictable as God leads. I choose to walk in great faith. I must move in circumstances in which I have no control. I will do so without fear. My faith is alive and well and brings forth great outcomes.

Prayer:

Lord, I choose to trust you. I admit that there have been many opportunities to take risks but in many instances, I chose the safe route. In this season, I choose to believe you in areas that I have not believed before. I relinquish control. I trust you completely and totally. Thank you for the great outcomes that will be seen in my life in the near future. I ask these things in Jesus' mighty name, Amen.

Personal Reflections:

Week Forty-Four

My Life Will Yield Much Fruit.

Scripture:
John 15:5-8

In this post pandemic era, it is very easy to disconnect from everything and everyone. Having to physically isolate from people for extended periods of time has facilitated in disconnection to an unhealthy extent. Now that restrictions have been relaxed, the effects of the global experience are yet evident. It is clear that it has become convenient to remain in isolation and in a state of disconnection. While we have been forced to reevaluate what and who we are attached to. We must never allow ourselves to be disconnected from God. We must make a daily decision to be permanently connected to God by way of Jesus who made everything possible. As we abide, dwell, and stay in Him, we become more engrafted each day. When you speak, He speaks. When you ask, Jesus asks the Father. Your life becomes fruitful and productive in ways that you have not ever imagined. Those who bear much fruit bring much glory to God. So as we proceed in this ever-changing era, we can determine to be healthy and bear healthy fruit.

Declaration:
I choose to stay committed to what's connected to God. By allowing Jesus to be Lord of my life, those circumstances and people change. I refuse to allow external variables to bring separation in

my relationship with God. My life will bring forth much fruit that glorifies God.

Prayer:
Dear Lord, thank you for the opportunity to stay attached and connected to you. Each day I will invest in my relationship with you. I am committed to you and I receive all that you are in my life. Thank you for making me a fruitful and powerful vessel in you. Amen.

Personal Reflections:
_____
_____
_____
_____
_____
_____
_____
_____
_____
_____
_____
_____
_____
_____
_____
_____
_____
_____
_____
_____
_____

Week Forty-Five

God Loves Me Unconditionally

Scripture:
1 John 4:18-19

It can take a long time for most people to conceptualize unconditional love, because most of us are accustomed to the conditional kind. It begins in our childhood. Many people are taught that love is distributed or experienced when the report cards look good or after the performances at school or church or in karate class or in sports or after recitals. God's love is not based on our performance. Unfortunately, many people are always waiting for the let down. So many people are often unable to really receive unconditional love because their experiences with love has had many strings attached to it. Their entire interaction is based on fear including, fear of rejection, fear of miscommunication, fear of conditions being unattainable, unreasonable, or simply inconvenient. It is completely freeing to know that God's perfect love casts out fear. So we can receive His love freely without fear of Him, without pressure and we can love Him without the fear of the let down. This is a whole game changer! God loves us no matter what we do and in spite of what we don't do. Nothing will ever change His love.

Declaration:
God loves me unconditionally. There may be consequences and rewards attached to my choices, but God will never stop loving me.

I receive God's love today and I am free to love Him without fear. God loves me just because I am.

Prayer:

Dear Lord, thank you for loving me regardless of what I do or don't do. Thank you for the ultimate expression of your love which was displayed when Jesus died on the cross to redeem us from the effects of sin. Thank you for enabling me to receive and experience the love of others unconditionally. Help me to demonstrate unconditional love as I interact with others. Thank you for your endless and boundless love. Amen.

Personal Reflections:

Week Forty-Six

Forgive And Move On

Scripture:
Philippians 3:12-14

What is the healthy response to disappointment, hurt, betrayal, or devastation? What should you do after someone has maliciously attacked you? What happens when you have been wrongfully accused, abused, or rejected? The answer to any of these scenarios is to forgive and move on. I know you are thinking, "but what you don't understand is what I have been through! " You are right but Jesus knows. The apostle Paul had been shipwrecked and thrown in dark dungeons with rodents, animals, and filth. Paul had been beaten, scorned, and left for dead. He was misunderstood and falsely accused and so much more. It never stopped him from completing his assignment on earth. Even so, Paul wrote about pressing forward. He moved on and said "forgetting those things which are behind and reaching forward to those things which are ahead." What you must do is move on. Yes, it happened. Yes, you've been hurt and disappointed. However, you don't have to stay in that hurt. Don't stay in that moment and don't be a prisoner to those awful experiences. Forgive. By the grace of God, and move on! Pack up and move! Close the chapter! Turn the page and rip it out if you like! Let's just move on! You'll be glad you did!

Declaration:

I refuse to linger around hurtful atmospheres, people, and experiences. This week I choose to consciously move forward. I will not continue to rehearse and perpetuate painful experiences, events, and interactions. I move forward to engage in productive activities in the Kingdom of God.

Prayer:

Thank you Lord, for the opportunity to recover. Thank you for bringing some painful experiences to an end. Thank you for healing me completely and totally. I have much to look forward to, thank you! Amen.

Personal Reflections:

_____
_____
_____
_____
_____
_____
_____
_____
_____
_____
_____
_____
_____
_____
_____
_____
_____
_____

Week Forty-Seven

My "Finallys" Are Showing Up

Scripture:
Isaiah 41:11-16

The Israelites had a tedious journey when the Prophet Isaiah communicated this prophetic message to them. They had already experienced much warfare and opposition when this message was delivered. They have encountered some battles because of their own disobedience and rebellion. Battles occurred because someone was opposing God's plan for them. Regardless of the reason, the battles were intense and continuous. God spoke to them and said that those who were contending with them would be brought down to disgrace. He said that their enemies would be brought to a place of being nothing. Surely you can relate to this scenario. You've been fighting all kinds of battles. You brought some of them on with some of your personal choices. Others have taken the place because of your commitment to God. Again, regardless of the cost, the battles have been ongoing. The good news is that you too, will see the end of the challenges . Your battles are coming to an end. Restoration is a process. Even the most difficult challenge will soon be a triumphant testimony and you will declare "finally!" You are about to rejoice. You will celebrate because God will deal with every opponent. Yes, every opponent! So prepare for your victory laps because the battles are coming to an end and you will exclaim and declare "my finallys are showing up!"

Declaration:

I am encouraged because my battles will not last forever. These current difficulties are coming to an end. I am victorious in every area because God is dealing with my opponents. I will rejoice because my "finallys "are going to be evident very soon.

Prayer:

Thank you Lord for sustaining me through seasons of warfare. Thank you for not allowing my opponents to have victory over me. Thank you for fighting for me and dealing with my enemies. I shall prevail! Thank you for this season of restoration. Amen.

Personal Reflections:

_____
_____
_____
_____
_____
_____
_____
_____
_____
_____
_____
_____
_____
_____
_____
_____
_____

Week Forty-Eight

I Choose To Be Free

Scripture:
John 8:31- 34

It is not uncommon for people to be unaware of things that keep them in bondage. When we think of the word bondage many images come to mind. We often envision literal weighted balls and chains and bands around body parts in such a way that restricts mobility . The kind of bondage that we are considering is not always visible. However, just because there are no physical ties does not mean that we are not bound. We can be bound emotionally, mentally, and spiritually. We are often tied to others' expectations, our own unrealistic expectations, and our own limitations. We can be tied by guilt, shame, constrictions in our own thinking, other people's words, and experiences. We can be bound to peoples preconceived notions, rumors, confabulations, and even ill-intended predictions, speculations, and judgments. The list can go on. The good news is that we do not have to be bound to anything that has not come from our Father. He sent His son Jesus to release us from anything that is destructive. However, it is up to us to accept and maintain our freedom. We must do that by deciding every day to abide in the presence of God. You must be diligent in guarding and protecting your freedom as well. It does require diligence and consistency. However, it must be done. Choose to walk in freedom in every aspect of your life. After all, your freedom has already been paid for.

Declaration:
Jesus paid for my freedom. I do not have to be bound by anything or anyone. I choose to embrace and experience freedom each and every day. I will guard my freedom and will not return to that place of bondage.

Prayer:
Thank you, Father, for sending your son, Jesus, to pay for my freedom from bondage, pain, and other negative thoughts. I will not negotiate about returning to whatever I have been set free from. Thank you for your grace, which enables me to abide in you and maintain my freedom. I thank you now, Amen.

Personal Reflections:
_____
_____
_____
_____
_____
_____
_____
_____
_____
_____
_____
_____
_____
_____
_____
_____
_____

Week Forty-Nine

God's Grace Is Always Enough

Scripture:
2 Corinthians 12:7-10

Everyone needs help, especially when we are dealing with difficult circumstances. We often ask God to remove the things or the people that create our adversities. God does not always respond to those requests because He knows what He has invested in us. He also knows that His desire is for us to access and depend upon His grace. We always have enough to conquer, to overcome, and to achieve victory when we walk in His grace. It is always enough. God's grace always makes us better. So it is never a problem to ask for more of God's grace. There is never a shortage and grace is always enough for us.

Declaration:
I can walk through anything with God's grace. I know if God doesn't remove me from the adversity or remove what is bothering me, then I know that His grace must be and will be enough. Grace is available and abundant, there is always enough of it and I am always enough in His grace.

Prayer:
Dear Lord, thank you for your sufficient grace. Thank you for leading me and guiding me through situations even when I feel like everything and everyone is against me. Thank you for being a shield

through the storm and bringing me to victory. Thank you for discernment and serenity. I will walk with you through all my obstacles because I know you will see me through. Thank you Lord for loving me and removing what needs to be removed. In Jesus' name, Amen.

Personal Reflections:

_____
_____
_____
_____
_____
_____
_____
_____
_____
_____
_____
_____
_____
_____
_____
_____
_____
_____
_____
_____
_____
_____
_____

Week Fifty

All Residue Must Go!

Scripture:
2 Corinthians 5:17

Sometimes we think that our walk with God is a one time experience or that our journey is the totality of two or three pivotal encounters. However, our journey is really an ongoing process. We should always engage in development and transformation. In Jesus, there are continuous washings. Every day living lends itself to dealing with some residue, some leftover issues that can be dealt with on a continuous basis. So you are a new creature when you ask Jesus to be Lord of your life. It is wonderful that He is always shaping and molding and washing us as we interact with Him each day.

Declaration:
This week I choose to allow God to wash me again and again. I am becoming all that I am destined to be on a day-to-day basis. I am being washed and rinsed every day by the word of God. The old me is through and I am walking into what is new.

Prayer:
Thank you Lord Jesus for making it possible for me to begin again. Thank you for continually washing me on my walk with you as I read and study your word. Even when some residue surfaces, I will be washed immediately. Thank you for the process of

transformation. I am grateful that no past or present sin will prohibit me from experiencing your best this week. I am a new creature in you! Amen.

Personal Reflections:

Week Fifty-One

The Lord Delivers Me From Every Evil Work

Scripture:
2 Timothy 4:17-18

The apostle Paul was closing out his letter to Timothy. He was giving some final words of instruction and encouragement. He recounts several experiences and testifies about what God has brought him through. He also gives some words of caution and marks some individuals who had presented great challenges for him. He spoke words of exhortation which indicated that he was looking out for Timothy and others who were coming behind him. He even made mention of how God delivered him out of the mouth of the lion when he was thrown in the lion's den. He explicitly speaks of how God has preserved and protected him so that the Kingdom work would be completed. Paul knew that he was a trailblazer. He knew that he was assigned to clear the path for so many that would follow behind him. He also knew that at the time of writing this letter, he was not finished with his assignment. So he not only spoke to Timothy, but he spoke to himself when he said that " the Lord will deliver me from every evil work." So look at yourself, look at where you are right now. Yes, there are things that could bother you. There are some dangers. There are some looming threats. There are even some people who may be making things difficult for you. But choose to continue just like Paul did, knowing that God will preserve you for Kingdom business.

Declaration:
I am safe wherever I am. I will not be overwhelmed, concerned or tormented by fear. The Lord delivers me from every demonic tactic, strategy, plot, plan, mechanism, trap or device. I will complete my divinely appointed assignments. I am preserved for Kingdom business and I will accomplish what I am sent to do.

Prayer:
Thank you Lord, for the assurance that you will protect me from any destructive attacks. Thank you for preserving me from all opponents who strive to prevent the completion of my divine assignments. I will continue to build your Kingdom so that others will find you and embrace their gifts and callings in you. I'll give you praise and glory in Jesus' mighty name, Amen.

Personal Reflections:

_____
_____
_____
_____
_____
_____
_____
_____
_____
_____
_____
_____
_____
_____

Week Fifty-Two

The End Of The Story Is The Most Important Part

Scripture:
Genesis 50:20

Everyone needs to read and study the entire story of Joseph. There are many twists and turns, dramatic crises and triumphs, suspenseful as well as predictable events during the course of his life. There are so many opportunities for many practical lessons that can be harvested and applied in our lives today. For the sake of our brief consideration, we will go straight to the most important part: the end. When we do that when reading other texts, it is difficult to really appreciate the truth of the end without understanding the various developments and processes that took place in the story. In this case, you can read the end of the story and get something very meaningful and tremendously beneficial from it. Joseph declared "you meant evil against me, but God meant it for good." Things had come full circle. The same brothers who threw him into a pit and left him for dead and stripped him of his prized possession, were now standing before him. Their actions altered the entire course of his life. In his elevated position, he was now the one who held their fate in his hands. He would save and preserve their lives. God had done so much in his life that he was able to demonstrate true love and forgiveness, which was accompanied by grace, mercy, and favor. After so much had gone on he had the opportunity to be vengeful and punitive, but he acknowledged that God had a plan that was so much bigger than any of them had ever realized along the way. As it is today, there are clear and distinct natural and spiritual enemies in our lives. The opportunities for us to take matters into our own hands are always before us. It is always prudent and wise for us to rest in the fact that God has the better plan. He will use the wicked deeds of others as opportunities to demonstrate His power. So never forget that the processes only build you. Each step in the process is significant for your development and progress. Ultimately, how your story ends is what is most important. Decide to finish well.

Declarations:
God is changing how my story will end. It will not end the way my antagonists desire. I will not be moved by obstacles and deterrents that occur along the way. I will be quick to forgive and allow God to do the rest. I will rest in knowing that He is a God of justice and recompense. I will make it to my place of elevation and favor and I will bless people as God gives opportunity.

Prayer:
Dear Lord, thank you for ordering my steps. Even though there may be obstacles and hindrances along the way, I know that you will see to it that I reach my place of destiny in due time. Thank you for the great plans that you have established for me before the foundation of the world. My promotion and elevation has already been written in the heavens. I thank you for ensuring that I will fulfill my purpose on the earth to bring you glory. Thank you for seeing to it that I am never helpless, never hopeless, and never powerless! Amen.

Personal Reflections:

www.ingramcontent.com/pod-product-compliance
Lightning Source LLC
Chambersburg PA
CBHW050259120526
44590CB00016B/2419